About God and Spiritual Healing

About God and Spiritual Healing

2nd Edition

Richard M. Grove

Second Edition

Wet Ink Books
www.WetInkBooks.com
WetInkBooks@gmail.com

About God and Spiritual Healing 2nd Edition
by Richard M. Grove

Cover Design – Richard M. Grove
Layout and Design – Richard M. Grove

Typeset in Garamond
Printed and bound in Canada
Distributed in USA by Ingram,
    – *to set up an account* – *1-800-937-0152*

Library and Archives Canada Cataloguing in Publication

Title: About God and spiritual healing / Richard M. Grove.
Names: Grove, Richard M. (Richard Marvin), 1953- author.
Description: 2nd edition.
Identifiers: Canadiana 20260130869 | ISBN 9781998324316 (softcover)
Subjects: LCSH: Spiritual healing. | LCSH: God (Christianity) | LCSH: Christian Science.
Classification: LCC BT732.5 .G76 2026 | DDC 234/.131—dc23

The book, *Science and Health with Key to the Scriptures,* by Mary Baker Eddy has had a profound healing effect on my body and life experience. One can find full information about Christian Science, Mary Baker Eddy, the Bible Lesson, Christian Science periodicals and much more at: — www.christianscience.com

Dedicated to
Mary Baker Eddy
the founder of
Christian Science.

Table of Contents:

Table of Contents

Introduction – p.

Introduction:

Let me start by introducing you to these five questions and answers that will dovetail into the topic of God and spiritual healing. One would have to say that the entire book, *Science and Health* is about God and spiritual healing. I hope you read that book.

All five questions and answers come from Chapter 14 – Recapitulation – page 465 of *Science and Health*. Every page of this chapter is of significant importance but there is no point in me quoting the entire chapter. Please look it up and study every page.

Question.—**What is God?** Answer.—God is incorporeal, divine, supreme, infinite Mind, Spirit, Soul, Principle, Life, Truth, Love. *S&H p. 465:8*

Question.—**What is the scientific statement of being?** Answer.—There is no life, truth, intelligence, nor substance in matter. All is infinite Mind and its infinite manifestation, for God is All-in-all. Spirit is immortal Truth; matter is mortal error. Spirit is the real and eternal; matter is the unreal and temporal. Spirit is God, and man is His image and likeness. Therefore man is not material; he is spiritual. *S&H p. 468:8*

Question.—**What is man?** Answer.—Man is not matter; he is not made up of brain, blood, bones, and other material elements. The Scriptures inform us that man is made in the image and likeness of God. Matter is not that likeness. The likeness of Spirit cannot be so unlike Spirit. Man is spiritual and perfect; and because he is spiritual and perfect, he must be so understood in Christian Science. Man is idea, the image, of Love; he is not physique. He is the compound idea of God, including all right ideas; the generic term for all that reflects God's image and likeness; the conscious identity of being as found in Science, in which man is the reflection of God, or Mind, and therefore is eternal; that which has no separate mind from God; that which has not a single quality underived from Deity; that which possesses no life, intelligence, nor creative power of his own, but reflects spiritually all that belongs to his Maker. *S&H p. 475:5*

Question.—**Do the five corporeal senses constitute man?** Answer.—Christian Science sustains with immortal proof the impossibility of any material sense, and defines these so-called senses as mortal beliefs, the testimony of which cannot be true either of man or of his Maker. The corporeal senses can take no cognizance of spiritual reality and immortality. Nerves have no more sensation, apart from what belief bestows upon them, than the fibres of a plant. Mind alone possesses all faculties, perception, and comprehension. *S&H p. 488:21*

Question.—**How can I progress most rapidly in the understanding of Christian Science?** Answer.—Study thoroughly the letter and imbibe the spirit. Adhere to the divine Principle of Christian Science and follow the behests of God, abiding steadfastly in wisdom, Truth, and Love. In the Science of Mind, you will soon ascertain that error cannot destroy error. You will also learn that in Science there is no transfer of evil suggestions from one mortal to another, for there is but one Mind, and this ever-present omnipotent Mind is reflected by man and governs the entire universe. You will learn that in Christian Science the first duty is to obey God, to have one Mind, and to love another as yourself. We all must learn that Life is God. Ask yourself: Am I living the life that approaches the supreme good? Am I demonstrating the healing power of Truth and Love? If so, then the way will grow brighter "unto the perfect day." Your fruits will prove what the understanding of God brings to man. Hold perpetually this thought,—that it is the spiritual idea, the Holy Ghost and Christ, which enables you to demonstrate, with scientific certainty, the rule of healing, based upon its divine Principle, Love, underlying, overlying, and encompassing all true being. *S&H p. 495:25*

Conclusions about Causation

These citations are also from Science and Health by Mary Baker Eddy. Taken together, these passages affirm that true causation rests wholly in divine Law, not in matter. Healing follows as fear-based erroneous beliefs are replaced with spiritual understanding and consciousness is awakened to divine Law, and effects yield naturally to the government of divine Life, Truth and Love.

"Maintain the facts of Christian Science, — that Spirit is God, and therefore cannot be sick; that what is termed matter cannot be sick; that all causation is Mind, acting through spiritual law. Then hold your ground with the unshaken understanding of Truth and Love, and you will win. When you silence the witness against your plea, you destroy the evidence, for the disease disappears. The evidence before the corporeal senses is not the Science of immortal man.

To the Christian Science healer, sickness is a dream from which the patient needs to be awakened. Disease should not appear real to the physician, since it is demonstrable that the way to cure the patient is to make disease unreal to him. To do this, the physician must understand the unreality of disease in Science.

Explain audibly to your patients, as soon as they can bear it, the complete control which Mind holds over the body. Show them how mortal mind seems to induce disease by certain fears and false conclusions, and how divine Mind can cure by opposite thoughts. Give your patients an underlying understanding to support them

*and to shield them from the baneful effects of their own
conclusions. Show them that the conquest over sickness, as well as
over sin, depends on mentally destroying all belief in material
pleasure or pain.*" Science and Health p. 417:10

"*Physicians should not deport themselves as if Mind were non-
existent, nor take the ground that all causation is matter, instead
of Mind. Ignorant that the human mind governs the body, its
phenomenon, the invalid may unwittingly add more fear to the
mental reservoir already overflowing with that emotion. Wrong
and right way Doctors should not implant disease in the thoughts
of their patients, as they so frequently do, by declaring disease to
be a fixed fact, even before they go to work to eradicate the disease
through the material faith which they inspire. Instead of
furnishing thought with fear, they should try to correct this
turbulent element of mortal mind by the influence of divine Love
which casteth out fear.*" Science and Health p. 180:11

"*The Christian Scientist finds only effects, where the ordinary
physician looks for causes. The real jurisdiction of the world is in
Mind, controlling every effect and recognizing all causation as
vested in divine Mind.*" Science and Health p. 379:4

God is NOT a Myth

Let me start this essay with these three citations from *Science and Health* by Mary Baker Eddy. Note that the text in the square brackets was inserted by me. I have included the unabridged citation in italics above each paraphrase. You will soon understand the significance of my edits once you have read the essay.

S&H 390:7-9 — *"It is our ignorance of God, the divine Principle, which produces apparent discord, and the right understanding of God restores harmony."*
Paraphrase – It is our ignorance of divine Law, the divine Principle, which produces apparent discord, and the right understanding of divine Law restores harmony.

S&H 330:11 — *"God is infinite, the only Life, substance, Spirit, or Soul, the only intelligence of the universe, including man."*
Paraphrase – Divine Law is infinite, the only Life, substance, Spirit, or Soul, the only intelligence of the universe, including man.

S&H 330:19 — *"God is what the Scriptures declare Him to be, – Life, Truth, Love. Spirit is divine Principle, and divine Principle is Love, and Love is Mind, and Mind is not both good and bad, for God is Mind; therefore there is in reality one Mind only, because there is one God."*

Paraphrase – Divine Law is what the Scriptures declare God to be, – Life, Truth, Love. Spirit is divine Principle, and divine Principle is divine Love, and divine Love is divine Mind, and divine Mind is not both good and bad, for God is divine Mind; therefore there is in reality one divine Mind only, because there is one God.

I do believe in God but I probably don't believe in the God that so many believe in. To me, that God of the masses is a myth. Some people believe in an anthropomorphic God that looks down on mortals from on high and bestows miracles, or not, according to God's divine edict. Another common myth that some believe in is that God is a punishing God, a vengeful God that inflicts pain and suffering for something that one has done wrong or because they are on the wrong side of a social or political issue. Another contrarian belief is in a God that might even forget that you and your problem even exist and it takes pleading, begging and rattling God to wake him up from his busy schedule to finally recognize your existence and finally provide the needed help you so deeply desire. None of these are even close to the God that I now know and turn to in times of trouble of any kind. Because the word "God" is so packed with misconceptions and misunderstandings I have grown to avoid using the word "God" if at all possible. I have grown into using the term "divine Law" as a substitute synonym. For me, on a linguistic level, the phrase "divine Law" meets all, or at least most, of my communication needs.

Decades ago I was a devout proselytizing atheist for about fifteen years because I did not understand the true nature of God / divine Law. Being an atheist was the only way I knew how to rebel against the myth of the anthropomorphic God that so much of society espouses as God. It was not until I earnestly returned to studying Christian Science that I finally started to understand that God was really divine Law, a set of demonstrable principles or axioms that I was able to wholeheartedly stop referring to myself as an atheist. After many years of reading, praying and thinking about the topic I was finally able to personally break the myth of the anthropomorphic God.

The God that I now know as divine Law is actually the seven synonyms that Mary Baker Eddy, the founder of Christian Science, gave us for God, namely; divine Life, Truth, Love, Principle, Soul, Spirit, Mind. They all have demonstrable laws of harmony, laws of love, friendship, unity, mercy, tolerance, forgiveness, etc, behind them. Divine Law and these synonyms and their principles, values, cannot be construed as person, place or thing. They can't be pleaded to, to solve your problems but like any principle, one can turn to those axioms to solve every type of problem whether it be physical, emotional, family or even financial difficulties.

As with the laws and principles of mathematics, that we know on the human level, we don't plead and beg mathematics to solve a simple or complicated problem when doing our taxes or figuring out a complicated angle of a roofline when designing a new house. We might pray and know that there "is" a correct answer to solving a problem. We might pray to know the answer will be revealed to us but there would be no point in pleading and begging for the correct answer to appear and then be disappointed or angry at the principles of mathematics for not solving the problem for us. The point is that we need to study and learn the principles of mathematics and then with confidence know, understand and demonstrate those principles to your specific needs.

Like any principle or law, we must grow in our trust and understanding of that principle so that we can more accurately and more quickly apply the unfailing principles to correct any problem we might have. If you want to build a large strong bridge you need to first study the principles of engineering, mathematics and design, and then with confidence apply those principles to the design of your bridge. If you want to write a long and elaborate symphony you might need to learn about the principles of music, rhythm and the harmonics of sound. If you want a harmonious life experience you need to study the principles of divine Life, Truth and Love and learn how to apply them to every life and body situation.

As a simple example, if you are having a difficult time with a store clerk that you deal with that maybe has a prickly personality; you might pray to know that he is governed by divine Law and the laws of divine Love and the principles of joy and congeniality. You can pray to know that the principles and laws of divine Spirit are in action now and always for you and him and you are both the joyous activity of divine Life's living. You can pray to know that nothing can interrupt the perfect axioms of divine Law and that you are both the expression and reflection of divine Love. With confidence and surety you can pray to know that divine Law's principles of brotherhood that govern all mankind can never be interrupted, diminished or disturbed.

I had exactly that situation demonstrated in my life. I was on my way to a small local store; because of my past experiences I was expecting an unfriendly response to my complaint about a service that was provided me by this company. On the way to the store I was worried about how I might make my point and leave with satisfactory results. All of a sudden I realized that I was expecting negativity and I had labeled the owner as a difficult, prickly mortal. Within the ten minute drive I made a total mental turnaround in my thinking and walked in to the store with a sincere expectation that the laws behind divine Principle would be manifested. I was confident that divine Love is the only principle that could ever be in action. I resolved to know that the principles of love behind divine Law would be demonstrated. Four minutes after arriving and explaining my situation the store owner and I resolved the situation with a totally amicable solution. All problems disappeared into a friendly congenial interaction. I left the store totally happy with the solution that he suggested and seemed happy with.

This is just a very small example of how turning to and knowing the principles of divine Law healed what might have been a difficult customer, store owner interaction. We have to know that the laws and axioms of divine Law are always in action to be implemented as long as we turn to and trust those principles wholeheartedly. We can always turn in confident prayer and reflect and express divine Law.

Mrs. Eddy reminds us on page 2 of her seminal work, *Science and Health*, that *"God is Love. Can we ask [divine Law] to be more? [Divine Law] is intelligence. Can we inform the infinite [divine] Mind of anything [divine Law] does not already comprehend? Do we expect to change perfection? Shall we plead for more at the open fount, which is pouring forth more than we accept? The unspoken desire does bring us nearer the source of all existence and blessedness."*

Mrs. Eddy did not teach us to plead to an anthropomorphic God to solve material problems. On page 275 Mrs. Eddy tells us *"All substance, intelligence, wisdom, being, immortality, cause, and effect belong to [divine Life, Truth, Love, Principle, Soul, Spirit, Mind] God."* All belongs to these divine synonyms and are available at any moment to solve any problem.

Aside from the anthropomorphic concept of what God is, I try to avoid gender specific pronouns to describe God. Divine Love is no more a "he" or a "she" than an "it". None of Mrs. Eddy's seven synonyms have a gender and so then neither can divine Law.

It is only because of a limiting linguistic tradition that Mrs. Eddy grew up with, in the 1800s, that she naturally used the limiting pronouns; He, Him and His. Despite this limiting gender specific pronoun that Mrs. Eddy uses all the way through her book, *Science and Health*, she knew only too well the myth of such an anthropological God. Even the risk of using the nouns Father, Mother God can lead a naive reader to think that Mrs. Eddy believed in an anthropomorphic God.

On page 470 of S&H, Mrs. Eddy reminds us that, *"Man is the expression of God's being"*, meaning that man is the expression of the principles of divine Law; divine Life, Truth, Love, Principle, Soul, Spirit, Mind. At the very best labeling God with a gender specific pronoun is a poor convenient metaphor for placing God in our lives.

"God is what the Scriptures declare Him to be, - Life, Truth, Love. Spirit is divine Principle, and divine Principle is Love, and Love is Mind, and Mind is not both good and bad, for God is [divine] Mind; therefore there is in reality one [divine] Mind only, because there is one God." Page 330 of S&H

It is so important to remember that man is not the expression and reflection of a so-called vengeful God. God is not a punishing, anthropomorphic God that can be pleaded to for specific results. God is not even a he, a she or an it. I hope that this helps to break the myth about what God is or is not. God is divine Law and divine Law is God.

Before I leave the topic, here is one more idea from Mrs. Eddy from page 116 of S&H, *"Christian Science strongly emphasizes the thought that God is not corporeal, but incorporeal, - that is, bodiless. Mortals are corporeal, but God [divine Law] is incorporeal."* We must remember and hold to the idea that we are the perfect expression and reflection of the one incorporeal divine Law and all of the attributes that go along with divine Law.

One time I was praying to know this about dear friends that emailed me to pray for them. The email explained that her and her husband had both been stricken with dengue fever. My first thought was to affirm that they were incorporeal, perfect reflections and expressions of divine Law. They were not the corporeal expression and reflection of any seeming material law or axiom dictated by a disease called dengue fever even though they had both been diagnosed by a doctor. A medical doctor, after all, could only ever know them as corporeal beings susceptible to a myriad list of material problems and threat of death from that diagnosis. My job was to pray for them and know emphatically that they were perfect un-violated spiritual ideas not mortals. They were the perfect demonstration of divine Life, the perfect manifestation of divine Law. I had to pray to know that they were the perfect knowing; they were the perfect understanding and the perfect demonstration of divine Law's perfection. The perfect strength in perfect action, the perfect manifestation of divine Law.

My friends lived in a country were dengue fever was common and often considered debilitating for many weeks and sometimes even fatal. In their area there was a constant nagging fear of this belief. They were not

Christian Scientists but I had prayed for them in the past to overcome so-called laws of matter. Within a day or two my friend emailed back reporting that she was back at work symptom free and her husband had embarked on a three day international trip that required him to fly to three countries with little rest for the duration. I was told later that he struggled with some symptoms for those three days but I continued to pray for him until I heard back, some days later, that he was safe and sound and well. The symptoms never returned.

The core or the foundation of my prayer was that they truly were incorporeal spiritual expressions and reflections of divine Law's perfection, and could not suffer from any corporeal belief. It took no pleading or begging to an anthropomorphic God to make things right. There was no hoping that an anthropomorphic God would finally hear our prayers and acknowledge their plight with a blessing of health. It was simply a matter of understanding, seeing, knowing, the principles, laws of divine Truth. The harmonious axioms of their being could never be interrupted. It is the knowing and mentally applying divine Law that heals.

I am so grateful for Christian Science and the teachings of Mary Baker Eddy.

Be Careful
What You Think and Hope For

I grew up in a Christian Science household, going to Sunday School all of the joy-filled years of my youth. I jokingly say that I escaped and became a devout proselytizing atheist for fifteen years before I returned to earnestly study Christian Science and became a Class Taught student.

There are many lessons that one learns as one progresses in one's metaphysical understanding. One lesson that I learned revolved around something that my father, also a Class Taught student of Christian Science, said to me in earnest one day. I can't think of what the context was but one time, many years ago, he said, "Be careful what you think and hope for." Only later in my life did I start to understand the metaphysical significance of this statement. What his comment alluded to was that we, in fact all mankind, are a manifestation of our thought, we are a product of our thinking, so we had better be careful of what we think and hope for. Later in my study of Christian Science I discovered what Mary Baker Eddy said on this topic, in so many different ways.

I began to understand what Mrs. Eddy had to say on page 209 of S&H, she says, "*Mind, not matter, is causation. A material body only expresses a material and mortal mind. A mortal man possesses this body, and he makes it harmonious or discordant according to the images of thought impressed upon it. You embrace your body in your thought, and you should delineate upon it thoughts of health, not of sickness.*" My father's comment that I should be careful of what I think or hope for started to form a fuller meaning for me.

Further in the same book, Mrs. Eddy gives us a cautionary note on page 393 of S&H, "*Stand porter at the door of thought. Admitting only such conclusions as you wish realized in bodily results, you will control yourself harmoniously. When the condition is present which you say induces disease, whether it be air, exercise, heredity, contagion, or accident, then perform your office as porter and shut out these unhealthy thoughts and fears. Exclude from mortal mind the offending errors; then the body cannot suffer from them. The issues of pain or pleasure must come through mind, and like a watchman forsaking his post, we admit the intruding belief, forgetting that through divine help we can forbid this entrance.*" I started to recognize the fundamental importance of these statements as axioms of Christian Science in how they related to my father's comment; "Be careful what you think and hope for."

I can't remember what great or small thing that I was thinking or hoping for that caused my father to make his comment but it must have been significantly negative enough for him to issue such a warning.

The reason that this comes to mind at this time is because my darling wife, a lifelong Class Taught student of Christian Science and manager of the Ontario

Committee On Publication, recently passed on after a two or three year protracted illness for which she diligently prayed and worked with a Christian Science practitioner.

We are taught in Christian Science that Christian Science, when properly applied, heals 100% of the time. I have had so many healings in my years of studying Christian Science that I cannot deny the fact that Christian Science does heal. I have even healings and given testimonies about recent healings since my wife passed on. Despite this assertion I can't stop wondering why my wife was not healed and in fact only seemed to steadily decline physically with this particular problem. No one could have studied or prayed more consistently than my wife. No one could have worked more diligently than my wife did with a Christian Science Practitioner / Teacher, so why was she not healed?

The phrase, be careful what you think and hope for, has continuously inserted itself into my thinking. One night recently I woke to remember something that my wife repeatedly said in different ways, at least 20 times over our 31 wonderful years of marriage, and that was, "I hope that I pass on before you." My mind keeps flipping back to the idea that we need to be careful what we think and hope for, you never know how it is going to manifest in your life experience. Linked to this caution about watching our thinking is the emphatic metaphysical truth that the body is not self-acting and the body and indeed our life experience, is a manifestation of our thought.

Mrs. Eddy reminds us that matter is a manifestation of mortal mind or in other words, a manifestation of our thought. On page 411 of *Science and Health* she says, "The procuring cause and foundation of all sickness is fear, ignorance, or sin. Disease is always induced by a false sense mentally entertained, not destroyed. Disease is an image of thought externalized. The mental state is called a material state. Whatever is cherished in mortal mind as the physical condition is imaged forth on the body."

I am still perplexed as to why my darling wife passed on. I still want an answer. My fear is that Christian Science Teachers and Practitioners are so afraid of the question, so afraid of being judged and afraid of self-judgment that they refuse to answer the question to me fully and directly? Is the Teacher / Practitioner afraid to put the blame squarely on the patient because they have a hidden, unrevealed material belief that they are cherishing and not willing to be free of? Or is the Teacher / Practitioner afraid to admit that they did not reveal a particular material belief that needed to be healed?

Is it simply erroneous speculation on my part for me to think that in Kim's case, that she was so burdened by the fear that she did not want to be left alone if I passed on first? My firm belief is that this fear drilled deep to her underlying material belief that divine Love was not going to always meet her every human need. My suspicion is that the Christian Science Teacher/Practitioner did not first recognize this fear and secondly did not heal that fear.

Something that I find very interesting about Kim's case is that she was always healed of pain. During the long period of decline she would from time to time find herself in pain. I was adamant in my insistence that she call her Practitioner no matter the time of day or night. Every time, and I literally mean every time, Kim was in pain she was relieved of the pain within very few minutes. A few times the healing of pain was so swift and dramatic that I called the practitioner back to say that she was peacefully sound asleep. The specificity of prayer for the pain was always met with healing. What fear or material belief was not recognized and reversed mentally that did not heal the underlying problem.

My deep belief is that every student of Christian Science is, has or will, ask this same question: Why was he, she, parent or friend not healed? If the Teacher / Practitioner does not have a sincere, deep and full answer we will continue to lose students and the movement will continue to dwindle and come to an end. It seems to me that every time a profoundly devoted Christian Scientist like Kim passes on, "unhealed" we lose more members, and soon we will be none. In our church auditorium that holds 1000 people, we recently had 4 people arrive for a service.

Before I finish with this topic I want to say that since Kim's passing I continue to study, pray and have a full expectation of healing. I have recently given three testimonies of healings that have taken place since Kim's passing three months ago, but this does not arrest my question of why was Kim not healed - the movement needs a clear full answer.

Life, Spiritual Growth,
and the Myth of All or Nothing

I have finally come to terms with the idea that life, at its core, needs to be about spiritual growth, whether one identifies as a Christian Scientist or not. Some people may not realise this at first. Others may resist it entirely, as I did for too many years of my own life. Sooner or later, often without realising it, we begin to ask deeper questions about existence, matter, spiritual healing, fear, and what it means to trust something beyond what we can see and measure with what we call our five physical senses.

Our study and implementation of Christian Science is about spiritual growth, growing closer in our understanding and relationship to God, divine Law. Nothing suggests, however, that suffering during our study and prayer is an essential part of the learning curve. Nothing suggests that spiritual growth is instantaneous or that it unfolds as an all or nothing process. Some individuals will learn the principles of divine Law and their relationship with divine Mind more quickly than others. The only essential aspect is that we keep on studying and praying and trusting that the divine laws and principles are there to guide our journey no matter how circuitous our path might be.

I have learned that the phrase "all or nothing" can sneak into spiritual progress in subtle ways. All or nothing thinking suggests that if healing is not immediate, if trust is not absolute, if the path includes detours, then we have failed. I do not believe that is how divine Love leads. I believe growth is real and that when we strive, that progress is inevitable. Mrs. Eddy has much to say about progress. You can start by reading her words on page 495:25 "Question. — How can I progress most rapidly in the understanding of Christian Science? Rudiments and growth Answer. — Study thoroughly the letter and imbibe the spirit. Adhere to the divine Principle of Christian Science and follow the behests of God, abiding steadfastly in wisdom, Truth, and Love." You might consider reading more of that citation.

When I was a child, I remember a conversation at the dining room table that has stayed with me for decades. My mother was surprised when her brother called to ask for the name and number of a Christian Science practitioner. My uncle had grown up in Christian Science but had been away from studying Christian Science ever since leaving Sunday School. Now he had a teenage boy who had a non-life threatening condition that was not yielding to medical assistance. My memory, now some sixty years later, tells me that my cousin was finally healed through working with the Christian Science practitioner. The thing that I find most interesting is that my uncle and his family did not continue to study Christian Science. Spiritual progress was not on their agenda when looking for a healing.

Even as a child, I sensed the strangeness of that. I did not have the words for it, but I sensed it. A spiritual healing had happened, and yet it did not become a door that opened onto a new way of life. It was as if someone had been pulled from a river and then walked away, grateful for the rescue, but not curious about the force that reached in and lifted them out. I am not judging my uncle. I am simply noticing something about human nature, and about my own nature. We can accept an outcome without accepting the implications. We can accept relief without allowing the relief to change our thought.

Another interesting example is that a dear non-Christian Science friend asked me if Christian Science could heal his prolonged and debilitating back problem that he had been taking painkillers and other medication for. I said yes and spent a bit of time explaining the value and premise of Christian Science to him and gave him the contact information for a practitioner that I have used. My friend reported to me that the back problem was healed with one treatment. I find it interesting that this friend did not turn the corner and start studying Christian Science. I recommended that he call a practitioner about a condition that his daughter suffered from. To the best of my knowledge he never did return to asking Christian Science for help.

There are other cases that I know personally but I will not bother citing them right now. To me it is all about the fear of giving up a belief even though there has been some evidence that Christian Science heals. It is easier to accept a healing as an exception than to let it challenge one's entire framework of thought.

I have watched this pattern enough times that I can no longer pretend it does not exist. The interesting thing is that I have watched this pattern even in myself. I can see and understand the temptation to treat Christian Science as an emergency service rather than a way of life that can be relied on. It is easy to call a Christian Science Practitioner when one is frightened, when one is desperate or when one has tried everything else but we don't want to let it change the base structure of our beliefs. It seems easy to not let it rearrange the assumptions that your life is based on and not let it challenge the deep habits of thought that say matter has power, and our material perception of time is a reality or physical symptoms are based in truth. Studying and praying is the real spiritual work, and it is the work that often feels slow.

At a Wednesday evening service at my branch church, we recently sang hymn 245. These words resonated with me; "If from that path we wander, and far astray we roam, oh call us faithful Shepherd, and bring us safely home." It struck me deeper than ever before that it is God, divine Law, the principles of being, that will bring us safely into harmony even if we wander from our spiritual path.

I do not know why those lines hit me so hard on that particular evening. Perhaps it was because I had been thinking about my own zigzags. Perhaps it was because I had been thinking about my uncle, and my friend, and how easily a healing can be received without a sustained change of thought. Perhaps it was because I had been thinking about the moments when I myself have wandered, not necessarily in outward behaviour, but in inward trust. There are days when I feel steady and clear, and there are days when I feel like my thought is divided. Those words remind me that the calling is not fragile. Divine Love does not say, You wandered, so now you are disqualified. Divine Love says, Come home. And it is the coming home that matters.

Don't be tempted by animal magnetism to give up your study of Christian Science and abandon your spiritual growth. If we feel like Christian Science, a Christian Science practitioner, or even our self has failed us because we have not seen a swift enough healing, it is not the time to give up our study and prayer in Christian Science.

If one turns to other means including medical help for a time, for relief from symptoms or pain, even while one continues to study Christian Science, then don't judge yourself or condemn Christian Science. It is simply part of your personal learning process. Study and spiritual growth is not an all or nothing process.

Mrs. Eddy reminds us on page 162:9 of S&H, *"The effect of this Science is to stir the human mind to a change of base, on which it may yield to the harmony of the divine Mind."* Stirring the human mind to a change of base sometimes takes time and is part of our ongoing personal process, but more importantly it always takes continued study and prayer.

That phrase, a change of base, has stayed with me. It suggests that the spiritual journey is not merely a series of improvements layered onto an old foundation. It is a foundation shift. It is not just learning new ideas, but being willing to let those ideas rebuild your sense of cause and effect. When I look honestly at my life, I see that much of my struggle has not been about whether Christian Science heals in principle. My struggle has been whether I will allow my base to change in practice. Will I let divine Law become more real to me than symptoms, more authoritative than fear, more governing than habit? That is a journey. That is growth and it is not all or nothing.

There is no time line for how we might grow spiritually. There are no rules that dictate if and when you should give up a long term or short term medication or have or not have a medical procedure. Study and prayer will show the way.

The fact is that Mrs. Eddy took a rather circuitous path through medical and alternative medical processes of her day before she arrived at her understanding of Christian Science. None of her journey disqualified her from continuing her spiritual study and arriving at a greater understanding of her true spiritual nature and gaining a greater ability to demonstrate the efficacy of Christian Science.

Sometimes slowly, sometimes quickly we will grow in our understanding that: page 95:30 of S&H "*Material sense does not unfold the facts of existence; but spiritual sense lifts human consciousness into eternal Truth.*" Spiritual growth is about lifting our human consciousness into a greater understanding of the spiritual truth that we are all spiritual beings now and always.

Mrs. Eddy reminds us on page 128:14 of S&H, "*A knowledge of the Science of being develops the latent abilities and possibilities of man. It extends the atmosphere of thought, giving mortals access to broader and higher realms.*"

Hopefully Mrs. Eddy's teachings will provide a somewhat shorter path for our spiritual growth, but there is not one single time line to overcome the belief that we are mortal. Most certainly our study is not an all or nothing process. For some, maybe most of us, it is a difficult belief to be rid of, that we are not mortal stuck in a material world with a material body but we are actually spiritual, the perfect reflection and expression of divine Law.

Mrs. Eddy reminds us, on page 261:4 of S&H, to, "*Hold thought steadfastly to the enduring, the good, and the true, and you will bring these into your experience proportionably to their occupancy of your thoughts.*"

I have come to love that instruction because it is both simple and demanding. It is not all or nothing. It implies the process of turning thought toward the enduring, the good, and the true. You keep returning to what you know of divine Law. You keep refusing to let fear become your guide. That is what steadfast means to me. It means I can be honest about my detours and still refuse to give up.

God does not stop loving us, or in other words, divine Law does not stop being true for you, just because you undergo a medical procedure, take a pain pill to alleviate painful symptoms, or if we take a seeming retrograde step. God's love for you is never ending, never waning. The laws and axioms of divine Law are always there right now and always for us to turn to as we hold thought steadfastly to the truth of being.

You can always turn back to the laws of divine Love that prove your true spirituality even if you have for a short or a long term turned to what seems like an alternate solution to solve a material problem. If you continue your study and prayer in Christian Science you will sooner or later learn that the laws of divine Life are permanent and forever available to everyone. Returning to study and prayer is always an option and should always be our goal.

A Christian Science practitioner once said to me (pardon this being a paraphrase), "If you ever revert to taking a pill or a medical procedure to alleviate negative physical symptoms or pain always mentally state that it is the power of mind that is doing the work not the pill or procedure. Matter has no power. Matter is never a cause or an effect and body is never self-acting."

The belief of the power of a pill, the belief of mortal mind, the belief of pain, the belief of suffering, are all the same false erroneous belief that man is mortal and not spiritual. Keep studying and praying to know that man is, that you are, now and always, the pure and perfect manifestation of divine Law. It does not matter how circuitous your journey is. It does not matter if you take a pill to alleviate the symptoms of pain, the truth is still and always will be the same. Your study and spiritual progress is not an all or nothing process.

I have had to learn to speak to myself with compassion here, and not with condemnation. Condemnation is one of the quickest ways to make the journey feel impossible. Condemnation says, You slipped, so it is over. Condemnation says, You took a pill, so you are a fraud. Condemnation says, Your healing was not quick, so you failed. None of that is divine Love. None of that brings freedom. Divine Law knows nothing of condemnation or shame. The principles of mathematics know nothing of condemnation or shame no matter how often we make a miscalculation. The principles of mathematics are simply always there for us to rely on. Divine Law is simply there for us to turn to and rely on no matter what mistakes we make on our path of spiritual growth. No matter what, we are still and always will be a perfect reflection of divine Law. It is just our job to recognise that truth as we grow spiritually.

I think it would be worthwhile that I mention my own case that happened in 2015. After many years of returning to Christian Science and having witnessed and experienced Christian Science healings, I had what my belief system considered a dire medical problem. It was not yielding to my studies and treatment in Christian Science. It did not yield to the treatment of a Christian Science practitioner.

I made the firm commitment to take myself to the emergency department at a local hospital. By then the condition was very painful and debilitating. After examinations I was rushed to another hospital for immediate surgery. The belief was so dire that I could pass on at any moment. My wife drove me immediately to the other hospital where they did further tests and rushed me into what was supposed to be a twenty minute surgery.

My wife was in the waiting room praying for almost three hours. What she did not know until later was that I had died on the operating table but was brought back to life. They finished the surgery and sent me to recovery with a foot long scar on my belly accompanied by other incision scars.

While I was immensely grateful for the surgical expertise and for being alive, I was most grateful for the ongoing prayers of my wife while I was on the operating table. After I survived the operation and the death experience I continued to pray and give myself treatment in Christian Science. With the care of home visiting nurses I was released from the hospital and recovered. All of that time I was praying. I was doing my metaphysical knowing that I was always, then and now, governed, guarded and guided by divine Law.

What I find interesting about my case is that despite the seeming success of the medical intervention I continued to pray and study Christian Science with some further examples of healings.

Despite my many healings in Christian Science I would on occasion feel despair and resort to medical or medicine assistance. A very recent example is that I went to bed after staying up much, much too late working on a writing project. I went to bed exhausted with the firm belief that I could suffer the consequences of over doing it. Sure enough I woke an hour and a half later to a headache. I sat in bed and prayed, listened to the Bible Lesson and read a few significant citations. Despite this metaphysical work the pain did not yield and I was too weary to continue praying. I took a painkiller pill and went back to sleep. The painkiller kicked in and I woke many hours later refreshed. Is this an all or nothing confession of failure?

What I find interesting is that I had a painkiller pill readily available to me in my night table. It is obvious that I had a belief in the power of the pill. As I mentioned earlier, it is the power of divine Mind not the power of the pill that does the healing. This is a bit of a tricky topic. I am not at all advocating that one should purposefully swing back and forth between a matter based solution and prayer. Mrs. Eddy makes it clear that this will get you nowhere.

Page 360:13 of S&H *"Dear reader, which mind-picture or externalized thought shall be real to you, — the material or the spiritual? Both you cannot have. You are bringing out your own ideal. This ideal is either temporal or eternal. Either Spirit or matter is your model. If you try to have two models, then you practically have none. Like a pendulum in a clock, you will be thrown back and forth, striking the ribs of matter and swinging between the real and the unreal."*

I admit that sometimes I feel like I am swinging like a pendulum but what I am suggesting is that if you falter in your understanding or even in your commitment that this is not the end of the spiritual growth journey for you. You can still and always return to demonstrating the efficacy of prayer.

Despite the seeming success of turning to a matter based solution I continue to pray and study. Mortal mind, the belief of a mind in matter, seems to tell me that there are a couple of mortal mind beliefs that are not yielding to my prayer and treatment in Christian Science but I persist in my studies, prayers and treatment.

Sometimes I am tempted to give up my trust in Christian Science all together but then I will remember a healing or in fact have a healing that I can only attribute to treatment in Christian Science.

Like my uncle and my dear friend I guess I am not about to switch gears and fully trust that Christian Science heals one hundred percent, one hundred percent of the time. Unlike my uncle and my friend I have had enough experience and demonstrations that I continue to pray and study and know that studying Christian Science is not all or nothing. I even pray and study that one day I will have one hundred percent trust and one hundred percent demonstration of the efficacy of Christian Science.

I want to say this carefully, because it matters. When I speak of one hundred percent trust, I am not talking about a human bravado that pretends fear or lack or pain does not exist in the human experience. I am talking about a deep trust that reflects our trust in divine Law that will carry us through, past and beyond what ever problem comes our way. A trust that is not rehearsed or comes from a citation but comes from faith and demonstration. Sometimes I have that pure sense of trust but sometimes I do not. I want to grow into a permanent trust and I believe that wanting it, and working for it, and returning to study and prayer, is itself part of the process of being stirred to a change of base and out of an erroneous belief.

This is where the two themes, "life and spiritual growth", and "all or nothing", meet in our experience. There is no doubt that life brings challenges, and challenges reveal what we actually believe. Sometimes I discover that my trust is strong. Sometimes I discover that my trust is conditional and sometimes I discover that my trust has a backup plan sitting in the bed side drawer. When I see that, I have two choices. I can judge myself, or I can treat it as progress. I can condemn, or I can learn and grow. I can call it failure, or I can call it an invitation to dive deeper into study and prayer and grow spiritually, after all growing spiritually is what it is all about.

I have an interesting testimony that illustrates the point that studying Christian Science is not an all or nothing process. This healing took place approximately in April 2021.

I had a rather miraculous healing of a very painful condition in my foot. About thirty years ago, before returning to my study of Christian Science, a doctor diagnosed a condition in my foot as being a bone spur on the back of my right heel. He said that the only way to fix the problem was through a minor medical procedure. Because the problem, at the time, was not particularly debilitating I chose just to ignore it and live with what was only occasional discomfort. From time to time I reverted to pain killers to get me through the day.

When I eventually returned to studying Christian Science, I prayed from time to time about the bone spur situation but there was never any permanent relief. Over the years the condition grew worse and worse to the point that I was in such pain that on some days I could hardly walk. One day the pain was so severe that I canceled an out of the office appointment for that day because I was literally not able to walk to the door let alone to the car. I continued to pray but over the following days the pain only subtly subsided and I was losing sleep.

Eventually I took a pain pill so that I could move around and think more clearly. I have to admit that taking the pain pill was far from full pain relief. The pain continued with no real tangible or permanent relief.

I should say that about three months before this severe pain I called a Christian Science practitioner and worked with him for many days. While I was very grateful for even the modest relief of pain I was very grateful for the spiritual guidance that I was receiving while working with the practitioner. I eventually stopped working with the practitioner somewhat discouraged that I did not have a full and profound healing, but I continued affirming two specific and very important ideas that the practitioner reminded me of very regularly. One was "the body is not self-acting" and the other was "everything is a manifestation of thought."

I had known both of those ideas from the many years that I had been studying Christian Science but for some reason they resonated with me much more than they ever had before. Coming to a better or more solid spiritual understanding of these parallel truths happened over that period I worked with the practitioner. I am so grateful for that spiritual learning experience.

In my ongoing metaphysical study, even while I took a pain killer, these two citations from *Science and Health* by Mary Baker Eddy supported those ideas: "*Disease is an image of thought externalized. The mental state is called a material state. Whatever is cherished in mortal mind as the physical condition is imaged forth on the body.*" page 411 S&H.

The other citation, also from *Science and Health* by Mary Baker Eddy, is, "*A change in human belief changes all the physical symptoms, and determines a case for better or for worse. When ones false belief is corrected divine Truth sends a report of health over the body.*" page 194 S&H.

From time to time I continued to take a pain pill. Even though I was somewhat discouraged by what seemed to be a fact that the pain was not totally healed, I continued to pray and stuck with those ideas that I was re learning, that "the body is not self-acting" and that "everything is a manifestation of thought." Even though on occasion I took a pain pill, I continued to pray and know that Christian Science does heal.

One day after being in debilitating pain for two or three weeks I was in my home office working. My cell phone rang in the other room. Without any consideration for the pain in my foot I jumped up from my desk and ran to get the phone. I quickly realized that I was moving without any pain. The pain was totally gone. Utterly and totally gone. It was like it had never been there. That was well over two years ago and I have been totally free from that condition ever since.

I continued to pray many other ideas that affirmed my spiritual oneness with divine Law, that I am not a mortal with a foot problem but a perfect spiritual idea of divine Love. I am fully governed, guided and impelled by divine Law.

I am so grateful for the spiritual growth that took place over the months and years of continued study and prayer. No retrograde step or temporary use of a pain pill disqualified me from growing spiritually. I am grateful for the prayerful support of the Christian Science practitioner that helped guide me on my journey of spiritual growth.

When I look back on that healing, I see how much it taught me about patience. I also see how it taught me about honesty. I was not pretending. I was not performing. I was not trying to appear spiritually impressive. I was in pain. I was tired. I was discouraged and yet something in me refused to let go of the spiritual facts I had been re-learning. Let me reiterate those two primary metaphysical truths that, "the body is not self-acting" and "everything is a manifestation of thought". Those ideas were not merely statements. They became anchors of truth that had shifted into understanding. Thank goodness life is a journey of spiritual growth and not an all or nothing axiom. Those ideas gave me something to stand on when my emotions were not steady.

What I am coming to see is that we are all on our own spiritual journeys through this belief in the reality of matter. My darling wife was a life-long, devout Christian Scientist and had many Christian Science healings but she passed on with a belief of cancer, Even in the struggle with that belief she studied and prayed fearlessly and passed on painlessly with a sense of peace and joy. That was her choice. That was the choice of my uncle and my dear friend, and it is my choice of how I sometimes struggle and demonstrate Christian Science.

I want to linger here, because it is easy to turn this kind of reflection into a debate. I do not want a debate. I am not trying to win an argument. I am trying to tell the truth about spiritual living as I have experienced it.

Every person's journey has its own texture. Some people have quick healings and slow growth. Some people have slow healings and profound growth. Some people have dramatic healings and then walk away. Some people have healings and return again and again, as I try to do. The important thing, to me, is not comparing, but continuing.

My wife's example remains precious to me. She was not naive. She was not in denial. She was not pretending that life is easy. She prayed with a kind of fearlessness that I still admire. She prayed with joy. She studied. She was sincere. She loved. Even in what the world calls an outcome of loss, there was something luminous in her way of being. I do not want to reduce her journey to a medical label. I want to honour her spiritual courage. I also want to learn from it. If she could pray joyously, then surely I can keep praying too, even when I feel uncertain.

As I write this, I realize that life, in general, is about spiritual growth and learning to reflect and express divine Law in every thought and action and overcoming the resistance that we find on the path. It is all about the purpose of being connected to divine Law and our never ending purpose of expressing divine Love. With that purpose in mind I call the process of spiritual growth learning how to do our knowing. We have to learn how to give ourselves and others treatment. Treatment is part of overcoming an erroneous belief and knowing the truth about reality. I suspect that my uncle and my friend had a healing but there was not much spiritual growth so they did not appreciate the healing as spiritual growth.

I have sat with that last thought many times. It may sound harsh on first reading, but I do not mean it as criticism. I mean it as observation. A healing can be received like a gift, but it can also be received like a step on the journey. If it is received like taking a pill, we rush back to what is our normal life as quickly as possible. If it is received like a gift, a step on the spiritual journey then we pause. We ask, What does this mean? What is being shown to me? How is my base being stirred? That pause is spiritual growth. The pause is where gratitude deepens into understanding.

When I say learning how to do our knowing, I mean learning how to think spiritually with purpose. Not merely repeating words and reading citations the way one might take a pill, but actually bowing to spiritual reality and recognising and stating that we are a perfect demonstration of divine Law. Prayer and treatment in Christian Science is not, and should not be thought of as a formula so please be cautious about thinking this is a definitive, singular method of praying or giving treatment but I have learned to give treatment in first person.

This is just a small, short, example of how I might give treatment for myself in first person: I am the perfect demonstration, the perfect reflection and expression of divine Law's omnipotent perfection. This problem (name the problem) is a lie of mortal mind. It (name the problem) is an illusions based in the idea that I am mortal. I am not mortal.

Add an infinite number of correct statements to your treatment as you progress day by day, hour by hour. I cannot have this problem (name the problem) because I am pure and perfect, upright, whole and free. I am the joyous activity of divine Life's living. I am the loved of divine Love's perfection now and always, never interrupted. I call some of these lines "mini treatments" that I state to myself as I move about in my day. I encourage everyone to write their treatment down and as they read and pray it take the opportunity to expand it with your own statements that you are learning from the Christian Science Bible Lesson or from your studies of *Science and Health* by Mary Baker Eddy.

This first person, affirmation and denial, treatment process affirms our perfect relationship to the omnipotent perfect, never interrupted divine Law. It denies that we are governed by fear, an illusion of mortal mind. I write these statements down and even store them in my phone because there are moments when I need to speak to myself clearly. I need to hear the truth stated in first person treatment form without apology. We have to overcome what mortal mind is suggesting is true. What mortal mind has to say can be loud, persistent and persuasive. It can claim that we are a vulnerable mortal body, that is at the mercy of biology and chemistry. When that kind of mental weather moves in, I have learned that I cannot negotiate with it. I have to deny it any sense of authority. We have to declare what is spiritually true, and I have to keep declaring it until the fear quiets.

In this joyous spiritual journey we will learn how to refuse the hypnotic insistence of symptoms, learning how to return to divine Law, not once, but repeatedly. Our journey is made of daily, hourly, returns. Mr. Eddy reminds us on page 322:3 of S&H "*When understanding changes the standpoints of life and intelligence from a material to a spiritual basis, we shall gain the reality of Life, the control of Soul over sense, and we shall perceive Christianity, or Truth, in its divine Principle.*"

And this, again, is where the all or nothing myth tries to interfere. If I declare the truth today and still feel afraid tomorrow, does that mean my declaration was useless? No. It means I am still being stirred. It means I am still changing base. If I pray today and still have symptoms tomorrow, does that mean prayer failed? No. It means I am still learning. It means I am still returning. If I have a moment of doubt, does that mean I have lost the whole path? No. It means I am on the path and I am growing.

I believe it is important to understand that sometimes healing is immediate, and sometimes it is not. Sometimes it comes like sunlight through a cloud break. Sometimes it comes like dawn, so gradual you only notice after the fact that the darkness has lifted. Sometimes it comes in a single moment like my foot healing, and sometimes it unfolds in stages, as thought yields. This is not to say that divine Law is variable. The unfoldment of the truth can seem variable. And yielding is not something we can force. It is something we consent to, again and again.

Page 417:10 from S&H *"Maintain the facts of Christian Science, - that Spirit is God, and therefore cannot be sick; that what is termed matter cannot be sick; that all causation is Mind, acting through spiritual law. Then hold your ground with the unshaken understanding of Truth and Love, and you will win."*

The phrase all or nothing can also show up as a demand that we must either rely only on Christian Science or rely only on medicine, as if we are not on a spiritual journey. My experience tells me that many people give up the erroneous beliefs about themselves slowly as they grow into understanding. The perfection of divine Law does not turn off and stop being divine Law for one person and not another. Do you remember learning the mathematical truth that 2+2=4. On the path to learning that, if you calculated incorrectly the first few times the principles of mathematics did not cut you off from ever knowing the truth.

So when I say, do not judge yourself, I mean it. Judgment hardens the heart and narrows the path. Judgment makes the spiritual journey feel like you are always on trial. Spiritual growth is not a trial, it is an unfoldment an awakening. Divine Law is not waiting with a clipboard recording our journey. Divine Law is present to lift consciousness into Truth. That is the mental work we must do.

Page 21:1 of S&H *"If Truth is overcoming error in your daily walk and conversation, you can finally say, "I have fought a good fight . . . I have kept the faith,"* because you are a better man.

This is having our part in the at-one-ment with Truth and Love."

I also believe that part of spiritual growth is learning how to interpret our own stories. We can interpret them as failure, or we can interpret them as learning. We can interpret them as proof that we are weak, or we can interpret them as evidence that we are being taught. We can interpret our detours as disqualification, or we can interpret them as part of the journey back. I believe the more loving interpretation is the more healing one. It is not indulgence. It is clarity. Divine Love leads with Love.

I think that is why hymn 245, that I mentioned earlier, moved me. The hymn does not pretend wandering does not happen. It acknowledges wandering. And then it asks for the call. It asks for guidance. It asks to be brought safely home. That is a prayer that does not shame itself. It simply asks. And it trusts that the Shepherd answers.

My hope in writing all of this is not to present myself as an example of perfect practice. I am not. My hope is to be honest about what it looks like to keep going. To keep studying and praying even when discouragement tries to make you stop. To keep returning even when you feel you have wandered. To keep trusting that divine Law is not a theory, but a present reality, governing, guiding, and impelling. That is what spiritual growth means to me. It is not a single heroic leap. It is a daily returning.

If an individual steps away after a healing, I do not judge them. I simply recognise that each of us is choosing, at every stage, what kind of meaning we will assign to what we experience. I want to choose meaning that leads to the perfection of divine Law and leads to deeper trust that knowing more about divine Truth will lead me to healing. I want to choose meaning that leads to a change of base and overcoming an erroneous belief that is holding me back from recognising my true spiritual nature.

Keeping the Window Open

With help from a Christian Science Practitioner friend I have slowly come to realise the importance of yielding to divine Law. I started to think of yielding to divine Law as simply opening the window and letting the breeze of divine Law's love enter into my life. This metaphor of opening a window helped me realise that all of the prayer and metaphysical studying that we do is simply the willing and humble process of opening the window to let in divine Law's ever present love. Once the window is open, once the willingness to think differently, it is our job to keep our thinking open through our ongoing commitment to prayer and study and then finally it is our job, as the perfect expression and reflection of divine Law, to simply yield to divine Law's ever present perfection.

I have often wondered what it means to 'yield' to divine Law. The dictionary says that 'yield' is simply 'to give way to'. Mrs. Eddy, the founder of Christian Science, reminds us in her book, *Science and Health*, that: "*All that really exists is the divine Mind and its idea, and in this Mind the entire being is found harmonious and eternal. The straight and narrow way is to see and acknowledge this fact, yield to this power, and follow the leadings of truth.*" S&H p.151

Further to this, Mrs. Eddy reminds us: "*This body is put off only as the mortal, erring mind yields to God, immortal*

Mind, and man is found in His image." S&H p.188. Mrs. Eddy refers to the importance of yielding, or giving way, to divine Law many times throughout her book *Science and Health with Key to the Scriptures.*

It is our job to joyously and calmly yield to the truths of divine Law, to give way, and be that perfect expression and reflection, the demonstration of divine Law. What does that perfect expression and reflection look like? It looks like health and normality. It can look like calmness and peace. It can even look like exuberant joy and jubilation but it always manifests as perfection from the grace of divine Law. All we have to do is open the metaphoric window and yield to divine Law, let the grace of divine Life, Truth and Love into our life.

Two simple examples of how opening the window to divine Law's grace come to mind. One example revolves around the healing of a headache that I had been struggling with for a day and a half. Finally on the second day I decided to lie down and have a snooze in hopes that this might relieve the symptoms. As I lay there unsuccessfully trying to sleep. I thought about the idea that I had been praying about; yielding to divine Law or in other words keeping the window open to divine Law's grace. I realized that sleep was not the answer. I lay there pondering divine Law's permanent, joyous love for me and that it was simply my job to yield to that Love by accepting, knowing that I am Pure, Upright, Whole and Free now and always. I remember that I was praying with other metaphysical truths that I had been learning but the idea of keeping the window open and yielding to divine Law's love kept coming to me. All of a sudden, without any struggle, I realise that I was not in any pain. I continued my day with joy celebrating that I am the joyous activity of divine Life's living.

I found this citation from *Science and Health* to be helpful. *"The Scriptures say, "In Him we live, and move, and have our being." What then is this seeming power, independent of God, which causes disease and cures it? What is it but an error of belief, – a law of mortal mind, wrong in every sense, embracing sin, sickness, and death? It is the very antipode of immortal Mind, of Truth, and of spiritual law. It is not in accordance with the goodness of God's character that He should make man sick, then leave man to heal himself; it is absurd to suppose that matter can both cause and cure disease, or that Spirit, God, produces disease and leaves the remedy to matter."*
S&H p.208

The other simple example is a healing of a rash on my hand. This rash was only a minor irritation and not at all debilitating but I could not help but see its seeming development of getting worse day after day. At the time I was working with a Christian Science practitioner about the same idea of, the importance of yielding to divine Law's perfection. I was literally working on the first paragraph of this article and praying to keep the window open when I glanced at my hand and noticed that there had been a dramatic diminishing of the rash. I don't know exactly when this had happened but I was surprised at the positive progress. The rash continued to diminish over the next few days until it was totally gone. It seemed to me to be perfect evidence of yielding to divine Law's grace. Both of these small and simple examples of healing were the result of keeping the window open to divine Law's love.

Mrs. Eddy reminds us that: "*As mortals reach, through knowledge of Christian Science, a higher sense, they will seek to learn, not from matter, but from the divine Principle, God, how to demonstrate the Christ, Truth, as the healing and saving power.*" S&H p.285

Don't Slam the Window Closed

If study, prayer and expressing divine Law are the processes of keeping the window open I guess we have to think about how it is that we are keeping the window closed.

One day I noticed that I was being disgruntled about something and realized that this is not a positive state of mind for keeping the window open. There is no grace in divine Law that allows for or creates a resentful or unhappy mental atmosphere. In fact it was quite the opposite, that mental state of mind was keeping the window slammed shut to the grace of divine Law.

We keep the window closed when we insist on expressing selfishness, worry, anxiety, irritation, anger, frustration, etc. All of these attributes are based in fear that divine Law will not meet all of our human needs. Being pugnacious, pedantic or argumentative will close the window to the perfection of divine Law being manifested in your life. The other way that we are keeping the window closed is by accepting the lie that we are mortal. If we accept, rather than deny, the reality of a material condition then we are keeping the window closed to accepting the grace of God. If we accept a material condition for others as a reality then we are also, inevitably, keeping the window closed.

I am not sure how else I am keeping the window closed but I think that I am starting to get the point.

Allowing divine Law to be divine Law

At a recent Wednesday evening Testimony Meeting a testifier said - that he had to learn to let God be God. Because I have been praying about the idea of "yielding" I put his comment in context with yielding to divine Law as being the only cause and creator and that his body was not a cause or creator and that he had to allow divine Law to be the only cause and creator – let divine Law be divine Law. This made me think of the daily prayer "Thy kingdom come, let the reign of divine Truth, Life and Love be established in me, …" The word "let" has become more significant to me lately. Get out of the way and "let" divine Law be divine Law and let divine Law do the governing. Don't get in the way of the fact that there is only one law, divine Law, one cause and creator.

Mrs. Eddy reminds us with these four important citations:

"Divine Mind is the only cause or Principle of existence. Cause does not exist in matter, in mortal mind, or in physical forms."
S&H p.254

"All substance, intelligence, wisdom, being, immortality, cause, and effect belong to God. These are His attributes, the eternal manifestations of the infinite divine Principle, Love. No wisdom is wise but His wisdom; no truth is true, no love is lovely, no life is Life but the divine; no good is, but the good God bestows."
S&H p.266

"There is but one primal cause. Therefore there can be no effect from any other cause, and there can be no reality in aught which does not proceed from this great and only cause. Sin, sickness, disease, and death belong not to the Science of being. They are the errors, which presuppose the absence of Truth, Life, or Love." S&H p.204

"Belief in a material basis, from which may be deduced all rationality, is slowly yielding to the idea of a metaphysical basis, looking away from matter to Mind as the cause of every effect. Materialistic hypotheses challenge metaphysics to meet in final combat." S&H p.268

I grew in my understanding that "yield" was a process or progression of honouring divine Law

Five Testimonies

Dear Reader: I am somewhat reluctant to include my testimonies at the end of this collection but I think it is important for the reader to understand that the truths found in Christian Science are demonstrable. Please recongise that I am a "student" of Christian Science. I am not a Christian Science "Practitioner" or a Christian Science "Teacher". I am not even close to being able to demonstrate the efficacy of Christian Science as the founder Mary Baker Eddy was. Please Read any one of the biographies on Mary Baker Eddy to glimpse a full understanding of her ability to heal. One of the many books that I can recommend you read is "Mary Baker Eddy: Christian Healer" (Amplified Edition) by Robert Townsend Warneck and Yvonne Caché Von Fettweis.

The healing efficacy of Christian Science is based on the healing truths, taught and demonstrated by Jesus. Mr. Eddy considered *"Jesus of Nazareth was the most scientific man that ever trod the globe. He plunged beneath the material surface of things, and found the spiritual cause."* S&H p.313

With this in mind I decided to add a few of my testimonies as examples of healings in Christian Science. It is often my habit to write down some of my testimonies, sometimes as emails to friends or sometimes in preparation for giving a testimony at church at a Wednesday evening testimony meeting. Here are just a few of my testimonies.

Hip Pain – Hospital Visit and a Spiritual Healing

It seems like a long strange journey but an example of a healing that I had is that one night I was suffering from a pain in my hip. This difficulty had been getting progressively worse over a period of two or three years. Over the years I had started to curb my activities so that I would not aggravate the situation with too much walking. By this time I was losing sleep, week after week, because of the pain. On occasion, in those weeks, so that I could sleep properly, I took a pain killer pill to alleviate the pain. During those difficult times neither the pain nor the pill prevented me from praying or continuing my metaphysical study of Christian Science.

One of my favourite metaphysical activities is listening to the Christian Science podcast program called "Sentinel Watch". This treatment came from my studies and my prayers. The foundation of this treatment is based on the writings by Mary Baker Eddy and was brought to light from listening to a "Sentinel Watch" podcast. I should point out that treatment in Christian Science should never be thought of as a formula but this is in part what I was praying with. This is not at all the full treatment.

> I am the perfect painless expression and reflection of the perfect divine Life, Truth and Love. I cannot be in pain because Life, Truth and Love are painless and I am the perfect

manifestation of divine Life, Truth and Love. Pain is not a physical condition; it is a mental condition, an erroneous false mental belief. Pain does not belong to me because pain is a lie, the father of illusion, claiming to be something. I am not in pain. I cannot be in pain. Pain is a counterfeit voice. The only true voice is the perfect joyous voice of divine Love. I am the loved of Love now and always. I am not in pain. There is no false belief. There is no false belief believer. I cannot even be tempted by a false belief. I cannot be in pain. I am the joyous painless loved of Love now and always.

After writing this treatment, praying, and studying different metaphysical writings I had a healing. I woke one night to a distressful noise in the other room and dashed to investigate. After realizing the noise was actually a false alarm, I realized that I was not in pain. I had painlessly lurched out of bed. Compared to the previous weeks I would have painfully sat up and slowly overcame the pain to stand and then tottered around for a few minutes until I was finally walking normally. Rejoicing in this pain-free experience I returned to bed and read and prayed the above treatment in celebration.

Well, I wish that was the end of the mortal mind dream but a couple of nights later, in the middle of the night, I was struck with so much crippling pain in the same hip that I could not move in any direction or even role over without agony. I could not even think of getting out of bed. At one point the pain was so severe that I wondered if this was a prelude to my passing on. Despite having taken a painkiller pill, after two or three hours of painful, fear-filled agony, I called for an ambulance to take me to the hospital.

At the hospital I was interviewed in agony, registered as a patient in agony, I was transferred to a wheelchair in agony and told to sit in agony until I was called. I sat and sat in agony for at least four hours. In the face of all of this pain I continued to pray asking myself these questions; Am I a mortal or immortal? As a spiritual idea can I possibly be subject to the illusion of pain? Is it even possible that I can be in pain if I am a manifestation of divine Law? Is God All-in-all?

During the long period after the ineffectual pain killer had long worn off, I still continued to pray. At some point I opened a file in my phone and read a treatment that I had written some time ago. The foundation of this treatment is based on the "Scientific Statement of Being" written by Mary Baker Eddy. The full "Scientific Statement of being" can be found on page 468 of her seminal book *Science and Health with Key to the Scriptures*, my treatment went like this:

> I am the perfect manifestation of divine Law's perfection because there is no life, truth, intelligence, nor substance in matter. I know that all is infinite divine Mind, Spirit and its infinite manifestation because divine Law is All-in-all. I am the perfect expression and

reflection of divine Law because Spirit is immortal Truth. I know that matter is mortal error and Spirit is the real and eternal. I know that matter is the unreal and temporal and that I am the perfect manifestation of divine Life, Truth and Love. I am the image and likeness of that perfection. I am not and all mankind, is not material. I am spiritual. I am not a mortal in pain. I am spiritual. I am a perfect reflection and expression of the one perfect divine Mind, now and always.

As I sat in utter agony I could hear a baby crying in pain. I instinctively gave my attention over to that dear child, knowing that the child and the parents were the perfect painless child of divine Love and perfection and that perfection can never be interrupted.

I prayed for the child for many minutes knowing that, they were also the perfect manifestation of divine Law's perfection because there is no life, truth, intelligence, nor substance in matter. I honestly don't know when the child became still and quiet because my attention was drawn to a moaning man yelling at three men sitting just across the aisle from him. He was demanding that they be quiet because he had been there for many hours, he was in pain and trying to sleep. Again I turned my attention to that dear man and mentally told him that he was in God's loving care, he was the loved of divine Love right now and always. Within 3 minutes a nurse came and took him into an inspection room and took care of him. I never saw or heard him again.

A short while later I woke, with absolutely no pain, to the sound of a man, a few feet from me, being called to an inspection room. Over my many hours of sitting and waiting I had notice him wincing in pain. Once again I had turned my thought to him as a pain-free loved of Love. The nurse called across the room asking if he needed any help with his wheelchair. He stood and said in a strong voice, "I don't even need the wheelchair." With joy in his voice he announced, "I am totally pain free, I will come right there." He stood and walked freely to where he was directed.

I sat for a few minutes continuing to pray that I too was a pain-free loved of Love. I continued praying the Scientific Statement of Being, knowing that I am the perfect expression and reflection of divine Law because Spirit is immortal Truth. I too was a pain free perfect expression of divine Law. I sat wondering what I should do. There were no nurses, no doctors or attendants in sight for ten or fifteen minutes. There were only patients sitting quietly so I wheeled myself outside to the curb. I sat in the morning sun feeling totally liberated and free. I rejoiced as a pain-free expression of diving Law as I read and prayed the treatment one more time.

Eventually I called over to a WheelTrans driver that was dropping off a patient and asked him to come and talk to me when he was free. I explained my situation that I had no shoes, no money and no way of getting home and did he have any suggestion of how I could get home. With a smile he said that he would drive me to my condo for free. He knew where my address was and in a very few minutes he pulled up to the front of my building where my wife met me with enough money as payment. Despite the man's refusal I gave him the payment with great thanks for rescuing me from my shoeless cool September morning wearing nothing more than shorts and a night shirt.

As it turns out, this time, this was the end of the mortal mind dream. After being dropped off by the kind driver, after a short catch up snooze, I had to go to my church to meet a contractor at a prearranged time. I worked hand in hand to solve a plumbing problem that had been a problem for some time. This so called hip problem gave me no trouble all day. That night I was able to sleep well with obvious progress that continued over the following hours. The next day after the hospital visit I was totally pain free and was up and down a ladder painting the ceiling in our bathroom. Now after two years I can say that I have been free of this hip problem ever since with no fear of a reoccurrence.

I am so grateful to Christian Science and the profound metaphysical work that Mrs. Eddy laid out for us in *Science and Health* and other of her many writings.

Thank you God for my life

Sometime in the early 2000 I was on Reading Room duty when a man came into the Reading Room all disgruntled about a brochure that we had in our Reading Room window that read: Suicide is Not the Answer.

He came in professing that suicide was the answer and he was planning on killing himself. I invited him to sit with me and talk. He spent many minutes ranting to me about how bad his life was, how painful his body was and that he had nothing to live for.

While he was ranting and bemoaning the miserable condition of his life I was praying to know that divine Mind, divine Love, would give me the right ideas to tell him. Eventually he calmed down and I explained a bit of how to get beyond all of the pain in his life. I knew I had to meet him on his level and brake through the crust of anger that he carried. The most important thing that we talked about was gratitude. He jumped on that right away and professed that he had nothing to be grateful for. I talked about all of the things that he can be grateful for; the blue sky, the green grass, his comfortable shoes, his next meal, etc. I finished my list of things to be grateful for with "Thank you God for my life. He balked and complained about that last item on the list. Eventually he was preparing to leave so I asked him if he would like me to pray that last item with him. With an uncommitted affirmation he said sure but he really was not grateful but if I wanted to that would be ok. I closed my eyed and simply prayed very slowly out loud "Thank you God for my life." With a long pause I then repeated that simple prayer. Three times I prayed it out loud and then I invited him to say it out loud with me. With reluctance he halfheartedly, with a bit of a flippant tone, he mumbled those words. With a long pause we prayed it out loud again. By the third time he was saying the words with more commitment in the tone of his voice.

I said before you leave I will give you that little prayer on a slip of paper. I carefully wrote it out "Thank you God for my life." I handed it to him and said that I wanted him to pray that prayer twenty times before you get to your bus stop. With great protest he complained and said "Twenty Times?" I said to him "You don't have anything to do so walk a few steps and stop and pray, Thank you God for my life. Walk a few more steps and pray it again.

That was the last I saw of him until about three months later Kim and I were going up an escalator and there was this man coming down. He pointed and waved at me, pulled that little slip of paper out of his shirt pocket and mouthed the words in silence to me "Thank you God for my life." My heart was filled with joy.

Then about three months later he showed up to a Wednesday Evening Testimony meeting at our church and stood up at the very back of the church with a microphone and said that a man in the Reading Room saved his life. He pulled out the little piece of paper and read "Thank you God for my life."

The Foot
on the Bathroom Counter testimony

At a Wednesday evening testimony meeting the First Reader read the story from John 9 that reminded us of the question, "Who did sin, the patient or the parents?" Jesus answered – "Neither hath this man sinned, nor his parents: but that the works of God should be made manifest in him."

For some reason it reminds me of a testimony from a couple of years ago that I like to call: The Foot on the Bathroom Counter testimony.

Laugh Out Loud! One might wonder about the joyous activity of putting one's foot up on the bathroom counter to clip one's toenails but for me recently, it was exactly that – a joyous activity.

Twice, about two years ago, I was so crippled with pain and swelling in my legs that the only way for me to move around our condo was in my office chair with wheels.

I was working with a practitioner that was accepting of my temporary use of non-prescription pain killers while we prayed.

As soon as I was able, I stopped using the pain medication. The entire time the practitioner worked with me he was knowing my pure and perfect spiritual wellbeing was always intact.

While working with the practitioner I had to re-learn a number of things.

One, was that the body is not self-acting.

Two, that the body is a manifestation of thought and Three, any seeming relief of pain from a pill is simply a placebo effect, a patient believes in the power of the pill, so it works.

As with the healing of the blind man, it was not me or my parents that sinned. The painful problem I seemed to be experiencing existed in thought only as a mortal belief not as a truth of my being.

Thank heavens I was not disqualified from the love of divine Love because I turned to the temporary use of a pain medication.

From Psalms, from the Responsive Reading in this week's Bible Lesson. It reads:

> "Unto thee, O Lord,
> do I lift up my soul.
> Remember not the sins of my youth,
> nor my transgressions:
>
> O Lord. O keep my soul, and deliver me:
>
> As for me, I will call upon God;
> and the Lord shall save me." end of quote.

For me I turned to knowing that I was and always will be loved by divine Love. It was an utter joy that I was permanently so pain free that I could stand on one foot and put the other foot up on the counter to clip my toe nails. For me it seemed like a spiritual miracle.

One + One = One

I re-learned a simple idea this week. We have all heard different versions of the metaphysical metaphor, 2 + 2 = 4. It is a metaphor for an immutable spiritual truth; for instance, "there is no reality in matter" or that "God is all-in-all". These truths are as true as 2 + 2 = 4. They are immutable. They can never be changed, perverted or compromised, they can always be relied on. Well another truth that I heard by email from my practitioner is that 1 + 1 = 1. I smiled when I read further and discovered why. "1 + 1 = 1 you and divine Law combine together as one. What a wonderful simple reminder that we are at one with divine Law, never separated. This immutable truth of our inseparability from divine Law can never be changed. Divine Law and I are one. This has always been and will always be the truth. As simple as that idea is, it was valuable for me to re-learn it in such a simple way.

That night I prayed with that simple idea; "1 + 1 = 1 you and divine Law. The next morning, for the first time in six weeks, I was able to pick my foot up high enough to step into the bathtub for a shower. Later in the day I was able, for the first time in as many weeks, to painlessly get in and out of the car unassisted. I mark my progress with re-learning this simple but powerful immutable truths. I thanked my practitioner for his prayerful support. I thank Mrs. Eddy our dear leader. I thank God or as I would rather say divine Law for me being permanently united as one.

Dental Surgery Testimony

There always seems to be plenty of opportunities to pray and demonstrate the efficacy of Christian Science. Last Wednesday evening I gave a testimony explaining that I was praying using a citation from the Christian Science Bible Lesson that quoted Mrs. Eddy's definition of church. In part it reads: "Church. The structure of Truth and Love." I applied that citation to myself stating that I was also the structure of divine Truth and divine Love.

This week I had an opportunity to pray, know and understand that truth once again. A few weeks ago I had a crown of a tooth pop off. I went to the dentist to have it glued back in place but they said it could not be done. They recommended surgery to remove the remaining root, more surgery to install a bone graph, followed by the installation of a dental post that would then hold a ceramic crown. A few days later I went to another dentist for a second opinion. After an examination, their opinion was exactly the same as the first. In the end the dentist that I chose was simply out of convenience for my own personal schedule. The two week time period before my appointment gave me plenty of time to pray about overcoming the fear of what was described as a small but complicated surgery. I continued to pray with the idea that I was the structure of Truth and Love. Expanding on that, I was the perfect, harmonious, painless, structure of divine Truth and Love. I continued to pray and expand on that idea over the following weeks before my appointment.

I also studied and prayed with a paraphrase that I wrote based on a citation from *Science and Health* on page 406:20. I can, and ultimately shall, rise as to avail myself in every direction of the supremacy of Truth over error, Life over death, and good over evil, and this growth will go on until I arrive at the fulness of divine Law's idea, and no more fear that I shall be sick and die. Inharmony of any kind involves weakness and suffering, — a loss of control over the body.

This is the full citation page 406:20: "We can, and ultimately shall, so rise as to avail ourselves in every direction of the supremacy of Truth over error, Life over death, and good over evil, and this growth will go on until we arrive at the fulness of God's idea, and no more fear that we shall be sick and die. Inharmony of any kind involves weakness and suffering, — a loss of control over the body."

Another citation that I prayed with and paraphrased is from page 428:23 – The evidence of my purity and perfection will become more apparent, as material beliefs are given up and the immortal facts of my being are admitted."

This is the full citation page 428:23: "The evidence of man's immortality will become more apparent, as material beliefs are given up and the immortal facts of being are admitted."

For me this meant, the evidence of my immortality, the evidence of my permanent painless perfection, will become more apparent as I give up the fear of dental surgery, and the material beliefs of the inevitability of pain with a lengthy recovery. I had to replace the fear with a confident understanding of the immortal facts of perfection that govern my being.

Even while reclined in the dental chair waiting for the dentist I continued to pray. When he arrived I was surprised at how vocally pessimistic he was when he was describing to his assistant how difficult the surgery was going to be and that he was afraid he was going to have to take the root out in three pieces. I continued to pray even while the surgery was underway. All of a sudden the dentist announced that the root extraction was finished and it came out in one piece. He announced to the dental student that was hovering over his shoulder that it was a surprisingly quick extraction. Within ten more minutes the bone graft and the post had been successfully implanted. They stitched me up and the procedure was quickly finished.

The dentist gave me a prescription for a week's worth of painkillers. I took one that night while I continued to pray that simple idea that I was the perfect, painless, structure of divine Truth and Love. In the morning I found only a slight discomfort and found no need to take any painkillers after that. On top of that the surgical wound healed remarkably quickly. Within two days, contrary to the pessimistic prediction from the dentist, I was eating almost totally normally and have had no problems ever since.

Here is another paraphrase that I also prayed with –
Every law of matter or the body, supposed to govern
me, is rendered null and void by the omnipotent
perfection of divine Law's permanent perfection.

This is the full citation page 380:32: "Every law of matter
or the body, supposed to govern man, is rendered null
and void by the law of Life, God."

I am so grateful that we can turn to our understanding
of Christian Science in any situation. No matter what
level of understanding we think we have, no matter
how few or great number of citations we might have
memorized, we can know that we are governed,
guarded and guided by divine Law. The permanent,
omnipotent perfection of divine Law is always there
for us to turn to. In our prayers, we pray, know and
understand many different truths. This idea from Mary
Baker Eddy's book, *Science and Health with Key to the
Scriptures*, is an important idea that I kept in mind is this
paraphrase base on the citation from page 402 – that
my life, harmony and perfection is established by divine
Mind. My so called material body manifests only what
I believe as true, whether it be a broken bone, disease,
or even the fear of dental surgery.

This is the full citation page 402:17: "The life of man is
Mind. The material body manifests only what mortal
mind believes, whether it be a broken bone, disease, or
sin."

Where to Find

You can find Christian Science at:
www.christianscience.com/

You can find verified testimonies at:
jsh.christianscience.com/testimonies

The last chapter of the book, *Science and Health with Key to the Scriptures*, is a chapter called Fruitage. It starts on page 600 to 700 and is testimonies by people that were healed by reading the book.

You can read *Science and Health* on line at:
www.christianscience.com/the-christian-science-pastor/science-and-health.

You can listen to the book, *Science and Health* for free at:
www.christianscience.com/listen-to-science-and-health?icid=Homepage:footer:Listen%20to%C2%A0S
cience%20and%20Health

You can learn about the book, *Science and Health* at:
www.christianscience.com/the-christian-science-pastor

You can read the book, *Science and Health* for free at:
www.christianscience.com/the-christian-science-pastor/science-and-health

www.ingramcontent.com/pod-product-compliance
Lightning Source LLC
Chambersburg PA
CBHW011240120626
46549CB00009B/3348